Dreams in the Bible

A Review of Every Dream in the Bible and its interpretation, plus a dream dictionary

L.F. McArdle

L.F. McArdle

Copyright 2018

Dreams in the Bible

All rights reserved. No part or portion of this book may be reproduced by any means without written permission from the author or author's agent, except for brief quotes containing reference to this book and author. This publication is protected under to copyright laws of the United States of America.

L.F. McArdle Copyright 2018

Dedication

This book is dedicated to the McArdle family.
May the Lord God Bless you all.

L.F. McArdle

"And he said, Hear now my words: If there be a prophet among you, I the LORD will make myself known unto him in a vision, and will speak unto him in a dream."

(Num 12:1)

Contents

Part I   A Biblical Foundation for Dreams   11

Part II   Biblical Dream Review   35

Part III   Dream Dictionary Launch Pad   121

Part I

A Biblical Foundation for Dreams

God Speaks Through Dreams   13

The Lord Contrasts Dreams with False Dreams   20

Caution Given To Believing Dreams and Dreamers   22

Dreams Are One Of The Revelatory Or Prophetic Gifts.   25

Dreams Are Scripturally Brought Into The New Testament and the Age of Grace   28

More Scriptures That Mention Dreams   29

Recording Your Dreams   30

Types of Dreams   31

Contents

Part II
Biblical Dream Review

Dream 1 King Abimelech's Dream 37

Dream 2 Jacob's Ladder Dream 41

Dream 3 Jacob's Dream of Cattle 45

Dream 4 Laban's Caution Dream 49

Dream 5 Joseph's Dream of Sheaves bowing down 53

Dream 6 Joseph's Dream of Sun, Moon and Stars 57

Dream 7 The Butler's Dream 59

Dream 8 The Baker's Dream 63

Dream 9 and 10 Pharaoh's Two Dreams 67

Dream 11 Midianite's Dream of a Barley Cake 73

Dream 12 Solomon's Dream 77

Dream 13 King Nebuchadnezzar's First Dream 81

Dream 14 King Nebuchadnezzar's Second Dream 89

Dream 15 Daniel's Dream 97

Dream 16 Joseph's First Recorded Dream 105

Contents

Part II

Biblical Dream Review

Dream 17 Wise men's Dream 109

Dream 18 Joseph's Second Dream 111

Dream 19 Joseph's Third Dream 113

Dream 20 Joseph's Fourth Dream 115

Dream 21 Pilate's Wife Dream 119

Part III

Dream Dictionary Launch Pad

- ❖ Animals 125
- ❖ Areas 129
- ❖ Body Parts 135
- ❖ Buildings and Places 139
- ❖ Colors 143
- ❖ Garments 149
- ❖ Numbers 153
- ❖ Objects 157
- ❖ People 161
- ❖ Vehicles 165
- ❖ Water 171
- ❖ Other Terms 175

Ample space is given to record your personal meanings and terms. All Scriptural References are from the authorized King James version of the Holy Bible.

Introduction

Years have passed since God has called me into the arena of understanding and interpreting dreams. I have met people that believed that dreams were divinely inspired and others that did not. Personally, I have found them to have unlocked many mysteries, and have taken my life and understanding into a whole new level. Dreams have helped me in many ways, one of them being, I am able to understand what my own dreams mean, as well as being able to teach others how to interpret their own dreams. Dreams can be prayed about which in turn can change a situation.

I believe many more people would be interested in dreams if only they knew that God was indeed behind them. I can't say for sure that every dream a person has is of God, however, to discount dreams altogether is foolish. God speaks in many different ways and dreams are one of those ways.

Introduction

Be it known; The New Testament book of James tells us to "be not many masters"; I do not profess myself as a master of dream interpreting; that would be in my estimate, the late John Paul Jackson. However, we felt lead to pass along our knowledge to help those that are interested in this subject. We trust it will be a blessing to you.

Acknowledgements

I want to acknowledge the following people and their families for various reasons, but mostly for their love and friendship. I appreciate having you in my life.

Andrea M.
Dale W. Sr.
Danny M.
Gerard M.
Larry I.
Mark N.
Martin M.
Matthew M.
Regina S.
Terry L.
Ursula T.
Walter M.
William and Minnie W.

Part I

God Speaks

Through Dreams

"And it shall come to pass afterward, that I will pour out my spirit upon all flesh; and your sons and your daughters shall prophesy, your old men shall dream dreams, your young men shall see visions:"

(Joel 2:28)

God Speaks Through Dreams

The Bible presents a challenge to man; Search me and find out why. Why things are the way they are, why God is the way he is, why we are the way we are, why is the world the way it is?

Dreams fall into this challenge. Search the scriptures and find out why there are dreams, how many different types of dreams, what is the purpose of dreams, what do objects, colors and animals symbolize in dreams and so on. To start with, we want to build a scriptural foundation that states God uses dreams as one method of speaking to mankind.

Sleep

Here is a thought to ponder: If an average person sleeps an estimated eight hours a night that would equate to one third of their twenty four hour day; if we took a sixty year old man and added up the number of hours he had slept in his lifetime it would therefore be a total of twenty years. God wants to use that time to speak to and therefore help that person; you and I included.

God Speaks Through Dreams

"And he said, Hear now my words: If there be a prophet among you, I the LORD will make myself known unto him in a vision, and will speak unto him in a dream." (Num. 12:1)

This scripture provides a way to know if a person is a true prophet: they receive visions and dreams.

This statement is from the Lord himself, found in the Old Testament book of Numbers. Using this single scripture we could actually stop right here having divine evidence that God indeed uses dreams; however we want to provide more divinely inspired words about dreams as they were recorded in the bible.

God Speaks Through Dreams

There are a few verses found in the book of Job that provides a more in depth reason for dreams and how they come; once again; these dreams and visions come from God:

"For God speaketh once, yea twice, yet man perceiveth it not. In a dream , in a vision of the night, when deep sleep falleth upon men, in slumberings upon the bed; Then he openeth the ears of men, and sealeth their instruction, That he may withdraw man from his purpose, and hide pride from man. He keepeth back his soul from the pit, and his life from perishing by the sword." (Job 33:14-18)

In the book of Job, we find a purpose for dreams and that most dreams come when we sleep. God speaks, or tries to get us to hear him, but for whatever reason we miss the message, so he tries again in a dream.

Sometimes He may send the same dream many times; (I have found that calling dreams and fear dreams have a flag of reoccurrence as a telltale sign).

God loves his creation, and desires for mankind to have a relationship with Him.

God may reach out to a person through a dream; however, if the individual is unaware that the dream is sent to cause a response from them to God then is it most likely discarded or regarded as just a memory to ponder.

Dream Example:

A man had a dream that he was walking down a hallway, off to the right was an open door to a bedroom; the room was dark with only the light from the hall shining inside, as he looked into the room he saw his wife asleep in a bed on the other side of the room, then a white gloved hand appeared in the middle of the room in midair holding an array of playing cards facing him, three of the cards had drifted up above the others and were floating there; they were jokers with faces of people he knew, then the dream was over.

Dream Test: If the dreamer can be removed from a dream and the dream still happens, then the dream isn't about the dreamer; in this case, if the dreamer was removed, the dream would not happen because there wasn't anyone else to see the hand of playing cards; therefore the dream is for him yet not about him.

The Interpretation: There are three people that are or will come in between you and your wife.

Needed Response:

1. Give God thanks for the dream

2. Pray that those three people would be removed from interfering with the relationship you have with your wife.

After the interpretation was given, he said that his wife had three siblings that would call and get her involved with their drama and she would get all worked up because of it.

A few days after he prayed the phone calls had completely stopped.

We also read why God does this:

1. *To withdraw man from his purpose.* (The will of a man may be in conflict with what God has desired for him/her. A dream can show us this).

2. *To hide pride from man.* (God gives dreams that can only come from him. Man cannot claim it was their great knowledge).

3. *To keep back his soul from the pit.* (God warns of immoral conduct through dreams, prompting us to change).

4. *Dreams can alert us of impending danger.* (The enemy has traps laid for our soul; God seeks to help man avoid them).

God Speaks Through Dreams

In the first book of Samuel we read of different ways in which God has been known to communicate. Dreams are mentioned.

"And when Saul inquired of the LORD, the LORD answered him not, neither by dreams nor by Urim, nor by prophets." (1 Sam 28:6)

"...And Saul answered, I am sore distressed; for the Philistines make war against me, and God is departed from me, and answereth me no more, neither by prophets, nor by dreams :..."   (1 Sam 28:15)

It is important to notice that God can stop giving dreams at any time, he did with King Saul. Those that despise a message from God may not get another one. This is to help us realize that God is not someone to take lightly. It is good to thank God for our dreams.

The Lord Contrasts Dreams with False Dreams

In the Book of the prophet Jeremiah, the Lord takes issue with people that were misleading others using dreams, he calls them false dreams.

False Dreams are one of the many categories of dreams. God wants us to be aware of this influence the devil has, so we can avoid believing the dream was from God.

Major indicators of a false dream are:

1. It leads us away from God or godliness. Anything that leads away from God is not of God.

2. It mocks the word of God; may present the law of God as not being true.

The Lord Contrasts Dreams with False Dreams

"I have heard what the prophets said, that prophesy lies in my name, saying, I have dreamed, I have dreamed. How long shall this be in the heart of the prophets that prophesy lies? yea, they are prophets of the deceit of their own heart; Which think to cause my people to forget my name by their dreams which they tell every man to his neighbour, as their fathers have forgotten my name for Baal. The prophet that hath a dream , let him tell a dream ; and he that hath my word, let him speak my word faithfully. What is the chaff to the wheat? saith the LORD. Is not my word like as a fire? saith the LORD; and like a hammer that breaketh the rock in pieces? Therefore, behold, I am against the prophets, saith the LORD, that steal my words every one from his neighbour. Behold, I am against the prophets, saith the LORD, that use their tongues, and say, He saith. Behold, I am against them that prophesy false dreams, saith the LORD, and do tell them, and cause my people to err by their lies, and by their

Caution Given To Believing Dreams and Dreamers

lightness; yet I sent them not, nor commanded them: therefore they shall not profit this people at all, saith the LORD." (Jer. 23:25-32)

Note: Some false dreams may also contain people appearing out of character.

Along with valuable items there comes an imitation, a bootleg if you will. Dreams are no different. God gives real dreams, true dreams and the devil gives false dreams. We must seek God for his input on how to interpret the dream, how to apply the dream as well as any other question we might have. It is wise to seek God's guidance at all times.

Caution Given To Believing Dreams and Dreamers

"If there arise among you a prophet, or a dreamer of dreams , and giveth thee a sign or a wonder, And the sign or the wonder come to pass, whereof he spake unto thee, saying, Let us go after other gods, which thou hast not known, and let us serve them; Thou shalt not hearken unto the words of that prophet, or that dreamer of dreams : for the LORD your God proveth you, to know whether ye love the LORD your God with all your heart and with all your soul. Ye shall walk after the LORD your God, and fear him, and keep his commandments, and obey his voice, and ye shall serve him, and cleave unto him. And that prophet, or that dreamer of dreams, shall be put to death; because he hath spoken to turn you away from the LORD your God, which brought you out of the land of Egypt, and redeemed you out of the house of bondage, to thrust thee out of the way which the LORD thy God commanded thee to walk in. So shalt thou put the evil away from the midst of thee." (Deut. 13:1-5)

Caution Given To Believing Dreams and Dreamers

If there is a dream that you have that is not good or that you do not want to happen, you can pray that the dream would not come to pass. The statement made by Jesus as he was praying: Thy will be done; is a wonderful preface or addition to any prayer we make;

Thy will be done but if I can make a request Lord, please don't allow that dream to come to pass; however you know what's best.

Dream Example

A father had a dream in which his two young boys were grown into teenagers; he saw they were both in gangs and doing drugs then the dream was over. He realized through the dream that he was neglecting his sons because of work; he adjusted his schedule and began spending time with them, they both became fine young men.

Dreams Are One Of The Revelatory Or Prophetic Gifts.

"And it shall come to pass afterward, that I will pour out my spirit upon all flesh; and your sons and your daughters shall prophesy, your old men shall dream dreams, your young men shall see visions:" (Joel 2:28)

This text found in the Book of the prophet Joel, has puzzled many believers. It states that old men shall dream dreams, and your young men shall see visions; however, there are plenty of young people, even children that had dreams from God so how can this be? Were the dreams given to the child not true?

The answer is found in how we read the scripture. There are three basic ways to approach a scripture;

1. Allegorical View, The verse or words are used as an allegory, Symbolic.

2. Literal meaning, which has the reader to accept this text as it is stated. It means what is

Dreams Are One Of The Revelatory Or Prophetic Gifts.

says. This is not always applicable For example:

" Ye are the salt of the earth: but if the salt have lost his savour, wherewith shall it be salted? it is thenceforth good for nothing, but to be cast out, and to be trodden under foot of men. Ye are the light of the world. A city that is set on an hill cannot be hid. " (Matt 5:13-14)

3. Deeper View, or Hidden View, much like other messages in prophetic or revelatory themes. They have a deeper meaning other than seen on the surface.

This scripture in the book of Joel 2:28, speaks of sons and daughters, and then old men and young men. The use of relatives is symbolic of the family of God.

"For whosoever shall do the will of my Father which is in heaven, the same is my brother, and sister, and mother." (Matt 12:50) also 1 Tim.5:1, 2

Old men and young men are seen as those that differ in age. Old age is symbolic of those

Dreams Are One Of The Revelatory Or Prophetic Gifts.

that are mature in spiritual matters, and young men are those that are immature. There are many young people that are very mature in spiritual matters, and unfortunately there are many older people that are immature in spiritual matters. God tends to relate with a person where there are spiritually.

"For every one that useth milk is unskilful in the word of righteousness: for he is a babe. But strong meat belongeth to them that are of full age, even those who by reason of use have their senses exercised to discern both good and evil." (Heb 5:13-14)

Mature people need to be challenged, or else they may become bored and disinterested. Personally, I went for many years desiring to be challenged by those that were over me in the ministry and never was fulfilled until God lead me into dream interpreting. Our dreams can challenge us, they cause us to think and search for answers. Visions are for the immature, the immature person can understand a vision, because a vision is what it appears to be.

Dreams Are Scripturally Brought Into the New Testament and the Age of Grace

On the day of Pentecost the Spirit of God was poured out upon a group of believers as recorded in the New Testament book of Acts chapter 2.

We read of a reference to the prophecy of Joel which includes dreams.

"For these are not drunken, as ye suppose, seeing it is but the third hour of the day. But this is that which was spoken by the prophet Joel; And it shall come to pass in the last days, saith God, I will pour out of my Spirit upon all flesh: and your sons and your daughters shall prophesy, and your young men shall see visions, and your old men shall dream dreams: And on my servants and on my handmaidens I will pour out in those days of my Spirit; and they shall prophesy:"

(Acts 2:15-18)

God was showing the world that He was doing something new, and that this new way was already spoken of.

More Scriptures That Mention Dreams

" He shall fly away as a dream, and shall not be found: yea, he shall be chased away as a vision of the night. "(Job 20:8)

Here we see dreams and visions of the night or night visions. Night visions differ from open visions because one occurs at night during sleep and the other can happen while we are awake.

"As a dream when one awaketh; so, O Lord, when thou awakest, thou shalt despise their image." (Ps. 73:20)

"When the LORD turned again the captivity of Zion, we were like them that dream." (Ps. 126:1)

" For a dream cometh through the multitude of business; ..."(Eccl. 5:3)

" For in the multitude of dreams and many words there are also divers vanities: but fear thou God." (Eccl. 5:7)

Recording Your Dreams

- Keep a pad and pen by the bed

- Have a soft light by the bed you can use quickly

- Date your pad before you sleep

- Write your dreams down as soon as you awake don't wait until later, dreams are known to vanish quickly.

- You may have many dreams in one night. (one night this man had six)

- Some dreams are on different levels: personal, local, regional, national and global.

- Review your dreams from time to time.

- Some dreams will convey the same message in different ways.

Types of Dreams

Let's take a look at the different types of dreams and their functions:

***Calling dream*-** This type of dream shows what God has called you to become or do; and or possibly the next step to becoming that. These type dreams are often reoccurring and mostly come at a young age. This type may be an answer to a prayer for guidance; especially to a student or a graduate.

***Caution Dream*-**Dreams that cause us to pay close attention to something, also called a warning dream.

***Correction dream*-** Dreams concerning ungodly behavior that we need to change.

"Likewise also these filthy dreamers defile the flesh, despise dominion, and speak evil of dignities." (Jude 8)

This type of dream may require the dreamer to repent and ask for forgiveness for their behaviour that was shown them.

Types of Dreams

Courage dream- This type of dream provides courage to do what God wants us to do;

Note: courage is only given when confronting a fear. The Lord knows what we have need of before we ask.

Direction dream- What God wants us to do next.

False dream- Usually involves people out of character

Fear dream-Many people experience fear dreams. This type of dream involves a fear that has us bound, or possibly even stopped. The purpose of this type of dream is set us free; we need to ask God for deliverance from this fear.

This type of dream is often reoccurring until conquered.

Types of Dreams

Invention dream - God gives people dreams that show a new idea, method or product. These ideas or inventions are sent to help solve problems and or raise the quality of life.

Many people have received songs, ideas and so on. One man who never wrote a song before told how that he received the words and the music to a song in a dream or vision.

Projection Dreams - We can also use the term fast forwarded; this type of dream usually involves conduct or a personal characteristic that has been projected in time to the place where it will take you if you continue with it.

Prophetic dream - Shows what is about to happen. Could be in the near future or distant future. If an item is near to you in the dream then it is soon to happen, but if the item is far away then it will happen in the distant future. Proximity is important in some dreams; saying this so you are aware.

Types of Dreams

Self awareness dream- Shows us our faults, flaws or unrighteous character

Spiritual warfare dream- What the enemy is doing to stop you.

Third party dream- These are dreams concerning others in order to help them. A key feature is that we have no active part in the dream, we are there to observe. We are not given dreams to damage a person or hurt them with the knowledge we get; we are entrusted with knowledge in order that we may know how to help.

Warning dream- Dreams that warn of impending danger

Word of knowledge dream- These are dreams that contain specific knowledge to help us; providing information that is important to unlock a situation.

Part II

Biblical

Dream

Review

"And there was there with us a young man, an Hebrew, servant to the captain of the guard; and we told him, and he interpreted to us our dreams ; to each man according to his dream he did interpret. And it came to pass, as he interpreted to us, so it was;"

(Gen 41:12-13)

Dream 1

King Abimelech's Dream

Bible Reference: *Genesis 20 1-9*

Dream Type: **Warning Dream**

This dream shows us a conversation that went on with God and King Abimelech. This record shows us that you can communicate in a dream, in this case the King was defending himself. Man's proud defense or justification is of little or no worth to God when it comes to His will being done. God stated that he knew what was said and that he didn't allow the King to touch the woman. Notice the ending; that God was not taking the King at his word, since he ended the conversation with what would happen if he touches her. God still respected man's free will to choose, however, it was made clear in a warning dream, the consequences that would follow if the warning was not heeded.

Dream 1

King Abimelech's Dream

Observations:

- ➢ God can affect the affairs of men by dreams.

- ➢ God can reveal our future.

- ➢ Dreams can inform us of an end of something. If we refuse to change our current conduct we know what will happen.

- ➢ God can reveal the truth no matter what we have been told.

"And Abraham journeyed from thence toward the south country, and dwelled between Kadesh and Shur, and sojourned in Gerar. And Abraham said of Sarah his wife, She is my sister: and Abimelech king of Gerar sent, and took Sarah. But God came to Abimelech in a dream by night, and said to

Dream 1

King Abimelech's Dream

him, Behold, thou art but a dead man, for the woman which thou hast taken; for she is a man's wife. But Abimelech had not come near her: and he said, Lord, wilt thou slay also a righteous nation? Said he not unto me, She is my sister? and she, even she herself said, He is my brother: in the integrity of my heart and innocency of my hands have I done this. And God said unto him in a dream , Yea, I know that thou didst this in the integrity of thy heart; for I also withheld thee from sinning against me: therefore suffered I thee not to touch her. Now therefore restore the man his wife; for he is a prophet, and he shall pray for thee, and thou shalt live: and if thou restore her not, know thou that thou shalt surely die, thou, and all that are thine. Therefore Abimelech rose early in the morning, and called all his servants, and told all these things in their ears: and the men were sore afraid. Then Abimelech called Abraham, and said unto him, What hast thou done unto us? and what have I offended thee, that thou hast

Dream 1

King Abimelech's Dream

brought on me and on my kingdom a great sin? thou hast done deeds unto me that ought not to be done." (Gen.20:1-9)

Dream 2

Jacobs Ladder

Bible Reference: *Gen 28:10-17*

Dream Type: Courage Dream

Jacob was a young man at this time, he had just left his parents house and was going out on his own. Following the advice of his father he was heading to a place to find a wife and start a family.
He was in the desert all alone and tired with his journey when he found a place to lie down and sleep. Jacob was no doubt dealing with some uncertainties of life. Then God gave him a dream.

We notice Jacob didn't say a word in the dream, God spoke and Jacob listened.
God introduced himself and stated what he would be doing for Jacob. What a great dream!

Dream 2

Jacobs Ladder

Observations

When God speaks it is for a good reason.

God was giving Jacob a dream he would not forget.
God stated five things He would do.

1. Bless Him
2. Bless his seed
3. Give him that land
4. Keep him
5. Be with him always

God provides dreams to encourage us in the days ahead. The times and trials may get rough, and we will need to draw on Gods promise. God has not changed. He still uses dreams as one way of encouraging us on our life's journey.

"And Jacob went out from Beer-sheba, and went toward Haran. And he lighted upon a certain place, and tarried there all night,

Dream 2

Jacobs Ladder

because the sun was set; and he took of the stones of that place, and put them for his pillows, and lay down in that place to sleep. And he dreamed , and behold a ladder set up on the earth, and the top of it reached to heaven: and behold the angels of God ascending and descending on it. And, behold, the LORD stood above it, and said, I am the LORD God of Abraham thy father, and the God of Isaac: the land whereon thou liest, to thee will I give it, and to thy seed; And thy seed shall be as the dust of the earth, and thou shalt spread abroad to the west, and to the east, and to the north, and to the south: and in thee and in thy seed shall all the families of the earth be blessed. And, behold, I am with thee, and will keep thee in all places whither thou goest, and will bring thee again into this land; for I will not leave thee, until I have done that which I have spoken to thee of. And Jacob awaked out of his sleep, and he said, Surely the LORD is in this place; and I knew it not. And he was afraid, and said, How dreadful is this place! this is none other but the house of God, and this is the gate of heaven."
  (Gen 28:10-17)

" He shall fly away as a dream, and shall not be found: yea, he shall be chased away as a vision of the night. "
(Job 20:8)

Dream 3

Jacob's Dream of Cattle

Bible Reference: *Gen 31:6-13*

Dream Type: **Knowledge Dream and Direction Dream**

Jacob had started a family which grew to considerable size, as he worked for years as a ranch hand. He was deceived by his father in law employer many times, yet God had blessed him with cattle for his own herd.

Life is not always about what we ourselves make of it.

If we obey God, he can change things around for our good. (Rom. 8:28)

Jacob submitted himself to his boss until the situation became too much for Jacob to bear any longer. God knew it was time for Jacob to move on.

Dream 3

Jacob's Dream of Cattle

Observations:

- ➤ God knows the hurts we suffer, and can reveal that facts, thus providing comfort.

- ➤ God can show us why things are the way they are.

- ➤ God can give directions for us to move from our current place.

" And ye know that with all my power I have served your father. And your father hath deceived me, and changed my wages ten times; but God suffered him not to hurt me. If he said thus, The speckled shall be thy wages; then all the cattle bare speckled: and if he said thus, The ringstraked shall be thy hire; then bare all the cattle ringstraked. Thus God hath taken away the cattle of your father, and given them to me. And it came to pass at the time that the cattle conceived, that I lifted up mine

Dream 3

Jacob's Dream of Cattle

eyes, and saw in a dream , and, behold, the rams which leaped upon the cattle were ringstraked, speckled, and grisled. And the angel of God spake unto me in a dream , saying, Jacob: And I said, Here am I. And he said, Lift up now thine eyes, and see, all the rams which leap upon the cattle are ringstraked, speckled, and grisled: for I have seen all that Laban doeth unto thee. I am the God of Bethel, where thou anointedst the pillar, and where thou vowedst a vow unto me: now arise, get thee out from this land, and return unto the land of thy kindred."
(*Gen 31:6-13)*

"Dreams are an invitation to know God"

Dream 4

Laban's Caution Dream

Bible Reference: *Gen 31:23-29*

Dream Type: Caution Dream

Laban had been Jacob's employer and then by marriage, became Jacob's father in law. Jacob was so upset at Laban for various reasons, that he and his family departed without saying goodbye to Laban. Laban was angered at Jacob and family's unannounced departure coupled with the discovery that one his idols was missing, commenced to pursue Jacob. Laban was very angry. On his way to confront his son in law, God speaks to him in a dream, causing him to be very cautious with his words when dealing with Jacob. I believe this was for Laban's sake. God was watching out for Jacob. We notice that Laban didn't say that God spoke to him in the dream, but that your father's God spoke to him in the dream. He had different gods.

Dream 4

Laban's Caution Dream

Observations:

- ➢ God can protect his people.

- ➢ God can humble a person with his power.

- ➢ God may speak to one person and not the other, even though the dream involves the other person.

'And he took his brethren with him, and pursued after him seven days' journey; and they overtook him in the mount Gilead. And God came to Laban the Syrian in a dream by night, and said unto him, Take heed that thou speak not to Jacob either good or bad. Then Laban overtook Jacob. Now Jacob had pitched his tent in the mount: and Laban with his brethren pitched in the mount of Gilead. And Laban said to Jacob, What hast thou done,

Dream 4

Laban's Caution Dream

that thou hast stolen away unawares to me, and carried away my daughters, as captives taken with the sword? Wherefore didst thou flee away secretly, and steal away from me; and didst not tell me, that I might have sent thee away with mirth, and with songs, with tabret, and with harp? And hast not suffered me to kiss my sons and my daughters? thou hast now done foolishly in so doing. It is in the power of my hand to do you hurt: but the God of your father spake unto me yesternight, saying, Take thou heed that thou speak not to Jacob either good or bad." (*Gen 31:23-29*)

Fear dreams are often reoccurring, prompting us to go to God in prayer for deliverance from that fear

Dream 5

Joseph's Dream of Sheaves Bowing Down

Bible Reference: *Gen 37:4-11*

Dream Type: Prophetic Dream

Joseph was the youngest of Jacob's family, yet he was rejected by his siblings. We all need love and attention from our parents and acceptance from our siblings. God was looking out for Joseph. God saw that his brothers would not speak peaceably to him, this had to hurt the boy. God blessed Joseph with a dream concerning sheaves. No one else was given a dream that we know of. It appears that the family was jealous of his dreams. Each brother was represented by a sheaf that was bowing down to his sheaf. This is the first dream with nothing but symbolism yet they knew what it meant.

Dream 5

Joseph's Dream of Sheaves Bowing Down

Observations:

- ➢ God loves to bless those that are despised and neglected.

- ➢ God can show us our future before we are there.

- ➢ God gives something to encourage us because the road ahead is rough and this will help sustain our spirit.

" And when his brethren saw that their father loved him more than all his brethren, they hated him, and could not speak peaceably unto him. And Joseph dreamed a dream , and he told it his brethren: and they hated him yet the more. And he said unto them, Hear, I pray you, this dream which I have dreamed: For, behold, we were binding sheaves in the field, and, lo, my sheaf arose, and also stood

Dream 5

Joseph's Dream of Sheaves Bowing Down

upright; and, behold, your sheaves stood round about, and made obeisance to my sheaf. And his brethren said to him, Shalt thou indeed reign over us? or shalt thou indeed have dominion over us? And they hated him yet the more for his dreams, and for his words." (*Gen 37:4-11*)

" For a dream cometh through the multitude of business; and a fool's voice is known by multitude of words."

(Eccl 5:3)

Dream 6

Joseph's Dream of Sun, Moon and Stars

Bible Reference: *Gen. 37:9-10*

Dream Type: Prophetic Dream

This is the second dream that contains only symbolism. In this dream , each member of the family unit is represented.

Notice the number of stars and the number of brothers, the sun, moon and stars are all part of a celestial family, symbolizing Joseph's family.

Joseph's father, Jacob knew what the dream meant. Some dreams are easier to interpret than others.

Dream 6

Joseph's Dream of Sun, Moon and Stars

Observations:

- ➤ God can send a message in different ways.

- ➤ God can use numbers as well as nature to show us a message, it is up to us to search out what it means.

- ➤ Dreams often go against logic and tradition.

"And he dreamed yet another dream , and told it his brethren, and said, Behold, I have dreamed a dream more; and, behold, the sun and the moon and the eleven stars made obeisance to me. And he told it to his father, and to his brethren: and his father rebuked him, and said unto him, What is this dream that thou hast dreamed? Shall I and thy mother and thy brethren indeed come to bow down ourselves to thee to the earth?"
(Gen. 37:9-10)

Dream 7

The Butler's Dream

Bible Reference: Gen 40:2-13

Dream Type: Prophetic Dream

The dream the butler had, showed him that the vine was before him, signifying it was in his future. (Position can be important)

Next he saw three branches; in this dream they were symbolic of three days, however here is an amazing event, the branches budded, blossomed and produced fruit.

Showing him that something miraculous would be happening that was not there before. Grapes grew for him to squeeze, then he had in his hand a cup, He was prepared for this moment to be a servant again to the Pharaoh.

Dream 7

The Butler's Dream

Observations:

➢ Dream interpretations belong to God.

➢ God may choose not to give an interpretation immediately, it is up to Him.

➢ In this dream 3 branches are symbolic of 3 days time.

➢ Some dreams are for the immediate future, and some are for the distant future, it all depends on the dream.

➢ The details are many but the theme is the most important part.

"And Pharaoh was wroth against two of his officers, against the chief of the butlers, and against the chief of the bakers. And he put them in ward in the house of the captain of the

Dream 7

The Butler's Dream

guard, into the prison, the place where Joseph was bound. And the captain of the guard charged Joseph with them, and he served them: and they continued a season in wards And they dreamed a dream both of them, each man his dream in one night, each man according to the interpretation of his dream, the butler and the baker of the king of Egypt, which were bound in the prison. And Joseph came in unto them in the morning, and looked upon them, and, behold, they were sad. And he asked Pharaoh's officers that were with him in the ward of his lord's house, saying, wherefore look ye so sadly today? And they said unto him, We have dreamed a dream , and there is no interpreter of it. And Joseph said unto them, Do not interpretations belong to God? tell me them, I pray you. And the chief butler told his dream to Joseph, and said to him, In my dream , behold, a vine was before me; And in the vine were three branches: and it was as though it budded, and her blossoms

Dream 7

The Butler's Dream

shot forth; and the clusters thereof brought forth ripe grapes: And Pharaoh's cup was in my hand: and I took the grapes, and pressed them into Pharaoh's cup, and I gave the cup into Pharaoh's hand. And Joseph said unto him, this is the interpretation of it: The three branches are three days: Yet within three days shall Pharaoh lift up thy head, and restore thee unto thy place: and thou shalt deliver Pharaoh's cup into his hand, after the former manner when thou wast his butler."
(Gen 40:2-13)

Dream 8

The Baker's Dream

Bible Reference: *Gen 40:16-22*

Dream Type: Prophetic Dream

This dream had terms that a baker can relate to, namely bread baskets and baked goods. Each basket represented a day. No doubt the baker baked a basketful per day for Pharaoh. The first two baskets were empty, and the third basket contained baked goods, however the birds were eating them. Birds are not usually a good sign in a dream, they fly in the air which is symbolic of spiritual beings that take things away, and they live among the trees. The position of these baskets being attached to the baker's head is a key. They represent an extension of him. This is not a good dream. Some dreams are not what we want to hear. We can always pray against it, this is called flipping a dream. This dream allowed the baker to get ready to die.

Dream 8

The Baker's Dream

Observations:

- ➢ Do not presume a dreams interpretation to be the same as someone else's.

- ➢ The words "I was in my dream" is a key: the dream was about him.

- ➢ Three baskets represented three days.

- ➢ God gave the baker time to repent.

" When the chief baker saw that the interpretation was good, he said unto Joseph, I also was in my dream , and, behold, I had three white baskets on my head: And in the uppermost basket there was of all manner of bake meats for Pharaoh; and the birds did eat them out of the basket upon my head. And Joseph answered and said, This is the interpretation thereof: The three baskets are three days: Yet within three days shall

Dream 8

The Baker's Dream

Pharaoh lift up thy head from off thee, and shall hang thee on a tree; and the birds shall eat thy flesh from off thee. And it came to pass the third day, which was Pharaoh's birthday, that he made a feast unto all his servants: and he lifted up the head of the chief butler and of the chief baker among his servants. And he restored the chief butler unto his butlership again; and he gave the cup into Pharaoh's hand: But he hanged the chief baker: as Joseph had interpreted to them."
(Gen 40:16-22)

Some dreams have delayed interpretations

Dream 9 and 10

Pharaoh's Two Dreams

Bible Reference: *Gen 41:1-28*

Dream Type: Prophetic Dream

Dream 9 Observations:

- Seven cattle were symbolic of seven years

- The health of the cattle symbolized agricultural conditions.

- River symbolized life itself how it keeps flowing.

- Lean cattle ate up the fat ones, symbolized sequence.

Dream 10 Observations:

- God used dream interpreting to get Joseph out of jail, and promote him.

Dream 9 and 10

Pharaoh's Two Dreams

- ➤ God still uses dreams to help us to be encouraged, to give us hope, to help us see a future.

- ➤ The ears of corn were symbolic of years

- ➤ The condition of being blasted was symbolic of: being attacked by, or stricken

- ➤ God gave these dreams to Pharaoh so he could prepare his nation.

"And it came to pass at the end of two full years, that Pharaoh dreamed: and, behold, he stood by the river. And, behold, there came up out of the river seven well favoured kine and fatfleshed; and they fed in a meadow. And, behold, seven other kine came up after them out of the river, ill favoured and leanfleshed; and stood by the other kine upon the brink of the river. And the ill favoured and leanfleshed kine did eat up the seven well favoured and fat

Dream 9 and 10

Pharaoh's Two Dreams

kine. So Pharaoh awoke. And he slept and dreamed the second time: and, behold, seven ears of corn came up upon one stalk, rank and good. And, behold, seven thin ears and blasted with the east wind sprung up after them. And the seven thin ears devoured the seven rank and full ears. And Pharaoh awoke, and, behold, it was a dream . And it came to pass in the morning that his spirit was troubled; and he sent and called for all the magicians of Egypt, and all the wise men thereof: and Pharaoh told them his dream ; but there was none that could interpret them unto Pharaoh. Then spake the chief butler unto Pharaoh, saying, I do remember my faults this day: Pharaoh was wroth with his servants, and put me in ward in the captain of the guard's house, both me and the chief baker: And we dreamed a dream in one night, I and he; we dreamed each man according to the interpretation of his dream . And there was there with us a young man, an Hebrew,

Dream 9 and 10

Pharaoh's Two Dreams

servant to the captain of the guard; and we told him, and he interpreted to us our dreams; to each man according to his dream he did interpret. And it came to pass, as he interpreted to us, so it was; me he restored unto mine office, and him he hanged. Then Pharaoh sent and called Joseph, and they brought him hastily out of the dungeon: and he shaved himself, and changed his raiment, and came in unto Pharaoh. And Pharaoh said unto Joseph, I have dreamed a dream , and there is none that can interpret it: and I have heard say of thee, that thou canst understand a dream to interpret it. And Joseph answered Pharaoh, saying, It is not in me: God shall give Pharaoh an answer of peace."

" And Pharaoh said unto Joseph, In my dream , behold, I stood upon the bank of the river: And, behold, there came up out of the river seven kine, fatfleshed and well favoured; and they fed in a meadow: And, behold, seven other kine came up after them, poor and very

Dream 9 and 10

Pharaoh's Two Dreams

ill favoured and leanfleshed, such as I never saw in all the land of Egypt for badness: And the lean and the ill favoured kine did eat up the first seven fat kine: And when they had eaten them up, it could not be known that they had eaten them; but they were still ill favoured, as at the beginning."

"So I awoke. And I saw in my dream , and, behold, seven ears came up in one stalk, full and good: And, behold, seven ears, withered, thin, and blasted with the east wind, sprung up after them: And the thin ears devoured the seven good ears: and I told this unto the magicians; but there was none that could declare it to me."

Dream 9 and 10

Pharaoh's Two Dreams

"And Joseph said unto Pharaoh, The dream of Pharaoh is one: God hath shewed Pharaoh what he is about to do. The seven good kine are seven years; and the seven good ears are seven years: the dream is one. And the seven thin and ill favoured kine that came up after them are seven years; and the seven empty ears blasted with the east wind shall be seven years of famine. This is the thing which I have spoken unto Pharaoh: What God is about to do he sheweth unto Pharaoh."*(Gen 41:1-28)*

Dream 11

Midianite's Dream of a Barley Cake

Bible Reference: *Judges 7:13-15*

Dream Type: Prophetic Dream

The Midianites had invaded the land and God chose Gideon to deliver Israel out from under their reign of terror. The dream was about a cake of barley bread that overthrew an army. A cake was typically small and round, barley was the grain for the poor, the wealthy ate wheat. This cake tumbled into the camp of Midian and smote a tent, it caused the tent to fall down and then it was overturned and lay along side. When something is smote or smitten it symbolizes having a very powerful effect on. The fall of the tent represented the destruction of the army of Midian.

The overturning of the tent means the reign of the army will be overturned and tossed by the way side of history, it is over.

Dream 11

Midianite's Dream of a Barley Cake

The cake of barley symbolizes Gideon's small army of poor people.

God uses things that are despised to bring to nothingness the things that are esteemed among men.

"But God hath chosen the foolish things of the world to confound the wise; and God hath chosen the weak things of the world to confound the things which are mighty; And base things of the world, and things which are despised, hath God chosen, yea, and things which are not, to bring to nought things that are:"

(1 Cor 1:27-28)

Dream 11

Midianite's Dream of a Barley Cake

Observations:

➢ God gave Israel's enemy a dream, which came by one man.

➢ God also gave the enemy the interpretation, which came by another man.

➢ God allowed Gideon to hear both, the dream and the interpretation, yet God didn't give the dream to Gideon directly.

" And when Gideon was come, behold, there was a man that told a dream unto his fellow, and said, Behold, I dreamed a dream , and, lo, a cake of barley bread tumbled into the host of Midian, and came unto a tent, and smote it that it fell, and overturned it, that the tent lay along. And his fellow answered and

Dream 11

Midianite's Dream of a Barley Cake

said, This is nothing else save the sword of Gideon the son of Joash, a man of Israel: for into his hand hath God delivered Midian, and all the host. And it was so, when Gideon heard the telling of the dream , and the interpretation thereof, that he worshipped, and returned into the host of Israel, and said, Arise; for the LORD hath delivered into your hand the host of Midian." *(Judges 7:13-15)*

Dream 12

Solomon's Dream

Bible Reference: *1 Kings 3:5-15*

Dream Type: Intercession Dream

This dream needs no interpretation. We put it in the category of intercession dreams because of what Solomon was doing.

He was in a place of trust over an entire nation at a very young age. He desired God to help him to know how to conduct himself and how to judge correctly, God granted his request.

God has been known to bless and be very close to young people that seek Him.

Dream 12

Solomon's Dream

Observations:

- Solomon interceded for himself, for wisdom to guide his country. God answered him in a dream.

- God loves to be inquired of.
  " And ye shall seek me, and find me, when ye shall search for me with all your heart."(Jer 29:13)

- Dreams can show us that nothing is too hard for God.

"In Gibeon the LORD appeared to Solomon in a dream by night: and God said, Ask what I shall give thee. And Solomon said, Thou hast shewed unto thy servant David my father great mercy, according as he walked before thee in truth, and in righteousness, and in uprightness of heart with thee; and thou hast kept for him this great kindness, that thou hast given him a son to sit on his throne, as it is this day. And now, O LORD my God, thou

Dream 12

Solomon's Dream

hast made thy servant king instead of David my father: and I am but a little child: I know not how to go out or come in. And thy servant is in the midst of thy people which thou hast chosen, a great people, that cannot be numbered nor counted for multitude. Give therefore thy servant an understanding heart to judge thy people, that I may discern between good and bad: for who is able to judge this thy so great a people? And the speech pleased the Lord, that Solomon had asked this thing. And God said unto him, Because thou hast asked this thing, and hast not asked for thyself long life; neither hast asked riches for thyself, nor hast asked the life of thine enemies; but hast asked for thyself understanding to discern judgment; Behold, I have done according to thy words: lo, I have given thee a wise and an understanding heart; so that there was none like thee before thee, neither after thee shall any arise like unto thee. And I have also given thee that which

Dream 12

Solomon's Dream

thou hast not asked, both riches, and honour: so that there shall not be any among the kings like unto thee all thy days. And if thou wilt walk in my ways, to keep my statutes and my commandments, as thy father David did walk, then I will lengthen thy days."

(1 Kings 3:5-15)

Dream 13

King Nebuchadnezzar's First Dream

Bible Reference: Dan 2:3-9 Dan 2:25-47

Dream Type: Prophetic Dream

This is another first in the Bible. A dream given to a king who was unable to recall it, was given again to Daniel along with the interpretation.

Showing us, that dreams given by God, are controlled by God.

Daniel makes it known to the king that interpreting a dream is a gift from God. Dreams are not meant to lift us up in pride but should humble us that we are being used to flow through to others.

Dreams come under the category of Prophetic gifts, or Gifts of The Holy Spirit.

Dream 13

King Nebuchadnezzar's First Dream

Observations:

- Daniel interpreted a dream that wasn't told.

- God can give a dream again to another.

- The dream was for that year and years to come.

- God was honoring Daniel with interpreting the dream.

- Daniel's humble character is seen as he gave God the Glory. Dreams are never to lift us up in pride.

" And the king said unto them, I have dreamed a dream , and my spirit was troubled to know the dream . Then spake the Chaldeans to the king in Syriack, O king, live for ever: tell thy servants the dream , and we will shew the interpretation. The king answered and said to the Chaldeans, The thing is gone from me: if

Dream 13

King Nebuchadnezzar's First Dream

ye will not make known unto me the dream , with the interpretation thereof, ye shall be cut in pieces, and your houses shall be made a dunghill. But if ye shew the dream , and the interpretation thereof, ye shall receive of me gifts and rewards and great honour: therefore shew me the dream , and the interpretation thereof. They answered again and said, Let the king tell his servants the dream , and we will shew the interpretation of it. The king answered and said, I know of certainty that ye would gain the time, because ye see the thing is gone from me. But if ye will not make known unto me the dream , there is but one decree for you: for ye have prepared lying and corrupt words to speak before me, till the time be changed: therefore tell me the dream , and I shall know that ye can shew me the interpretation thereof."(*Dan 2:3-9)*

"Then Arioch brought in Daniel before the king in haste and said thus unto him, I have found a man of the captives of Judah, that will

Dream 13

King Nebuchadnezzar's First Dream

make known unto the king the interpretation. The king answered and said to Daniel, whose name was Belteshazzar, Art thou able to make known unto me the dream which I have seen, and the interpretation thereof? Daniel answered in the presence of the king, and said, The secret which the king hath demanded cannot the wise men, the astrologers, the magicians, the soothsayers, shew unto the king; But there is a God in heaven that revealeth secrets, and maketh known to the king Nebuchadnezzar what shall be in the latter days. Thy dream , and the visions of thy head upon thy bed, are these; As for thee, O king, thy thoughts came into thy mind upon thy bed, what should come to pass hereafter: and he that revealeth secrets maketh known to thee what shall come to pass. But as for me, this secret is not revealed to me for any wisdom that I have more than any living, but for their sakes that shall make known the interpretation to the king, and that thou mightest know the thoughts of thy heart.

Dream 13

King Nebuchadnezzar's First Dream

Thou, O king, sawest, and behold a great image. This great image, whose brightness was excellent, stood before thee; and the form thereof was terrible. This image's head was of fine gold, his breast and his arms of silver, his belly and his thighs of brass, His legs of iron, his feet part of iron and part of clay. Thou sawest till that a stone was cut out without hands, which smote the image upon his feet that were of iron and clay, and brake them to pieces. Then was the iron, the clay, the brass, the silver, and the gold, broken to pieces together, and became like the chaff of the summer threshingfloors; and the wind carried them away, that no place was found for them: and the stone that smote the image became a great mountain, and filled the whole earth.

This is the dream ; and we will tell the interpretation thereof before the king. Thou, O king, art a king of kings: for the God of heaven hath given thee a kingdom, power, and strength, and glory. And wheresoever the

Dream 13

King Nebuchadnezzar's First Dream

children of men dwell, the beasts of the field and the fowls of the heaven hath he given into thine hand, and hath made thee ruler over them all. Thou art this head of gold. And after thee shall arise another kingdom inferior to thee, and another third kingdom of brass, which shall bear rule over all the earth. And the fourth kingdom shall be strong as iron: forasmuch as iron breaketh in pieces and subdueth all things: and as iron that breaketh all these, shall it break in pieces and bruise. And whereas thou sawest the feet and toes, part of potters' clay, and part of iron, the kingdom shall be divided; but there shall be in it of the strength of the iron, forasmuch as thou sawest the iron mixed with miry clay. And as the toes of the feet were part of iron, and part of clay, so the kingdom shall be partly strong, and partly broken. And whereas thou sawest iron mixed with miry clay, they shall mingle themselves with the seed of men: but they shall not cleave one to another, even as iron is not mixed with clay. And in the days

Dream 13

King Nebuchadnezzar's First Dream

of these kings shall the God of heaven set up a kingdom, which shall never be destroyed: and the kingdom shall not be left to other people, but it shall break in pieces and consume all these kingdoms, and it shall stand for ever. Forasmuch as thou sawest that the stone was cut out of the mountain without hands, and that it brake in pieces the iron, the brass, the clay, the silver, and the gold; the great God hath made known to the king what shall come to pass hereafter: and the dream is certain, and the interpretation thereof sure.

Then the king Nebuchadnezzar fell upon his face, and worshipped Daniel, and commanded that they should offer an oblation and sweet odours unto him. The king answered unto Daniel, and said, Of a truth it is, that your God is a God of gods, and a Lord of kings, and a revealer of secrets, seeing thou couldest reveal this secret." *(Dan 2:25-47)*

Not all dreams have a wonderful message

Dream 14

King Nebuchadnezzar's Second Dream

Bible Reference: *Dan 4:4-28*

Dream Type: Prophetic Dream

God was showing the king what he was about to do.

This presents a challenge for Daniel, he may die if the king gets upset at the interpretation, yet he still has to tell it.

Not all dreams have wonderful messages. Daniel knew that the king needed to humble himself and that is what the dream was about. If the king would have humbled himself and turned from his unrighteous deeds, then God could have changed the decree against him and his kingdom. This goes along with 2 Chron. 7:14.

Dream 14

King Nebuchadnezzar's Second Dream

Observations:

- ➤ The great tree was symbolic of a great leader. One who has great influence.

- ➤ Hewn down is symbolic of: to humble, to make low.

- ➤ The purpose for the dream is given in the dream.

- ➤ That God rules over all the affairs of men, or he has the final say. That is why prayer matters.

" I Nebuchadnezzar was at rest in mine house, and flourishing in my palace: I saw a dream which made me afraid, and the thoughts upon my bed and the visions of my head troubled me. Therefore made I a decree to bring in all the wise men of Babylon before me, that they might make known unto me the interpretation of the dream. Then came in the magicians, the astrologers, the Chaldeans, and

Dream 14

King Nebuchadnezzar's Second Dream

the soothsayers: and I told the dream before them; but they did not make known unto me the interpretation thereof. But at the last Daniel came in before me, whose name was Belteshazzar, according to the name of my god, and in whom is the spirit of the holy gods: and before him I told the dream , saying, O Belteshazzar, master of the magicians, because I know that the spirit of the holy gods is in thee, and no secret troubleth thee, tell me the visions of my dream that I have seen, and the interpretation thereof. Thus were the visions of mine head in my bed; I saw, and behold a tree in the midst of the earth, and the height thereof was great. The tree grew, and was strong, and the height thereof reached unto heaven, and the sight thereof to the end of all the earth: The leaves thereof were fair, and the fruit thereof much, and in it was meat for all: the beasts of the field had shadow under it, and the fowls of the heaven dwelt in the boughs thereof, and all flesh was fed of it. I saw in the visions of my head upon my bed,

Dream 14

King Nebuchadnezzar's Second Dream

and, behold, a watcher and an holy one came down from heaven; He cried aloud, and said thus, Hew down the tree, and cut off his branches, shake off his leaves, and scatter his fruit: let the beasts get away from under it, and the fowls from his branches: Nevertheless leave the stump of his roots in the earth, even with a band of iron and brass, in the tender grass of the field; and let it be wet with the dew of heaven, and let his portion be with the beasts in the grass of the earth: Let his heart be changed from man's, and let a beast's heart be given unto him; and let seven times pass over him. This matter is by the decree of the watchers, and the demand by the word of the holy ones: to the intent that the living may know that the most High ruleth in the kingdom of men, and giveth it to whomsoever he will, and setteth up over it the basest of men. This dream I king Nebuchadnezzar have seen. Now thou, O Belteshazzar, declare the interpretation thereof, forasmuch as all the wise men of my kingdom are not able to make

Dream 14

King Nebuchadnezzar's Second Dream

known unto me the interpretation: but thou art able; for the spirit of the holy gods is in thee. Then Daniel, whose name was Belteshazzar, was astonied for one hour, and his thoughts troubled him. The king spake, and said, Belteshazzar, let not the dream , or the interpretation thereof, trouble thee. Belteshazzar answered and said, My lord, the dream be to them that hate thee, and the interpretation thereof to thine enemies. The tree that thou sawest, which grew, and was strong, whose height reached unto the heaven, and the sight thereof to all the earth; Whose leaves were fair, and the fruit thereof much, and in it was meat for all; under which the beasts of the field dwelt, and upon whose branches the fowls of the heaven had their habitation: It is thou, O king, that art grown and become strong: for thy greatness is grown, and reacheth unto heaven, and thy dominion to the end of the earth. And whereas the king saw a watcher and an holy one coming down from heaven, and saying, Hew the tree down,

Dream 14

King Nebuchadnezzar's Second Dream

and destroy it; yet leave the stump of the roots thereof in the earth, even with a band of iron and brass, in the tender grass of the field; and let it be wet with the dew of heaven, and let his portion be with the beasts of the field, till seven times pass over him; This is the interpretation, O king, and this is the decree of the most High, which is come upon my lord the king: That they shall drive thee from men, and thy dwelling shall be with the beasts of the field, and they shall make thee to eat grass as oxen, and they shall wet thee with the dew of heaven, and seven times shall pass over thee, till thou know that the most High ruleth in the kingdom of men, and giveth it to whomsoever he will. And whereas they commanded to leave the stump of the tree roots; thy kingdom shall be sure unto thee, after that thou shalt have known that the heavens do rule. Wherefore, O king, let my counsel be acceptable unto thee, and break off thy sins by righteousness, and thine iniquities by shewing mercy to the poor; if it may be a lengthening

Dream 14

King Nebuchadnezzar's Second Dream

of thy tranquility; All this came upon the king Nebuchadnezzar."

(Dan 4:4-28)

One feature of the book of Daniel is prophecy by way of dreams.

Dream 15

Daniel's Dream

Bible Reference: *Dan 7:1-8:1*

Dream Type: Prophetic Dream

This dream is loaded with symbolism. We gain a great deal of understanding of dream language from the Bible. This is the last dream in the Old Testament

"So he told me, and made me know the interpretation of the things. These great beasts, which are four, are four kings, which shall arise out of the earth."(Dan.7:16-17)

Dream 15

Daniel's Dream

Observations:

➢ Daniel wrote his dream down. It is a sign of appreciation and value.

➢ This dream goes along with the Book of Revelation.

The last dream (#14) was of a leader being represented as a tree. In this dream four leaders are represented as four beasts. Trees provide food, a beast eats flesh.

The term Beast is symbolic of man eaters, (lion, bear, leopard and terrible) they destroy mankind. Evil

The sea is symbolic of the sea of humanity.

Dream 15

Daniel's Dream

" In the first year of Belshazzar king of Babylon Daniel had a dream and visions of his head upon his bed: then he wrote the dream , and told the sum of the matters. Daniel spake and said, I saw in my vision by night, and, behold, the four winds of the heaven strove upon the great sea. And four great beasts came up from the sea, diverse one from another. The first was like a lion, and had eagle's wings: I beheld till the wings thereof were plucked, and it was lifted up from the earth, and made stand upon the feet as a man, and a man's heart was given to it. And behold another beast, a second, like to a bear, and it raised up itself on one side, and it had three ribs in the mouth of it between the teeth of it: and they said thus unto it, Arise, devour much flesh. After this I beheld, and lo another, like a leopard, which had upon the back of it four wings of a fowl; the beast had also four heads; and dominion was given to it. After this I saw in the night visions, and behold a fourth beast, dreadful and terrible, and strong exceedingly;

Dream 15

Daniel's Dream

and it had great iron teeth: it devoured and brake in pieces, and stamped the residue with the feet of it: and it was diverse from all the beasts that were before it; and it had ten horns. I considered the horns, and, behold, there came up among them another little horn, before whom there were three of the first horns plucked up by the roots: and, behold, in this horn were eyes like the eyes of man, and a mouth speaking great things.

I beheld till the thrones were cast down, and the Ancient of days did sit, whose garment was white as snow, and the hair of his head like the pure wool: his throne was like the fiery flame, and his wheels as burning fire. A fiery stream issued and came forth from before him: thousand thousands ministered unto him, and ten thousand times ten thousand stood before him: the judgment was set, and the books were opened. I beheld then because of the voice of the great words which the horn spake: I beheld even till the beast

Dream 15

Daniel's Dream

was slain, and his body destroyed, and given to the burning flame. As concerning the rest of the beasts, they had their dominion taken away: yet their lives were prolonged for a season and time. I saw in the night visions, and, behold, one like the Son of man came with the clouds of heaven, and came to the Ancient of days, and they brought him near before him. And there was given him dominion, and glory, and a kingdom, that all people, nations, and languages, should serve him: his dominion is an everlasting dominion, which shall not pass away, and his kingdom that which shall not be destroyed. I Daniel was grieved in my spirit in the midst of my body, and the visions of my head troubled me. I came near unto one of them that stood by, and asked him the truth of all this. So he told me, and made me know the interpretation of the things. These great beasts, which are four, are four kings, which shall arise out of the earth. But the saints of the most High shall take the kingdom, and possess the kingdom for ever,

Dream 15

Daniel's Dream

even for ever and ever. Then I would know the truth of the fourth beast, which was diverse from all the others, exceeding dreadful, whose teeth were of iron, and his nails of brass; which devoured, brake in pieces, and stamped the residue with his feet; And of the ten horns that were in his head, and of the other which came up, and before whom three fell; even of that horn that had eyes, and a mouth that spake very great things, whose look was more stout than his fellows. I beheld, and the same horn made war with the saints, and prevailed against them; Until the Ancient of days came, and judgment was given to the saints of the most High; and the time came that the saints possessed the kingdom. Thus he said, The fourth beast shall be the fourth kingdom upon earth, which shall be diverse from all kingdoms, and shall devour the whole earth, and shall tread it down, and break it in pieces. And the ten horns out of this kingdom are ten kings that shall arise: and another shall rise after them;

Dream 15

Daniel's Dream

and he shall be diverse from the first, and he shall subdue three kings. And he shall speak great words against the most High, and shall wear out the saints of the most High, and think to change times and laws: and they shall be given into his hand until a time and times and the dividing of time. But the judgment shall sit, and they shall take away his dominion, to consume and to destroy it unto the end. And the kingdom and dominion, and the greatness of the kingdom under the whole heaven, shall be given to the people of the saints of the most High, whose kingdom is an everlasting kingdom, and all dominions shall serve and obey him. Hitherto is the end of the matter. As for me Daniel, my cogitations much troubled me, and my countenance changed in me: but I kept the matter in my heart." *(Dan 7:1-8:1)*

Both Old Testament and New Testament have recorded dreams.

Dream 16

Joseph's First Recorded Dream

Bible Reference: *Matt 1:20-25*

Dream Type: Instruction Dream

Looking back in Bible history, there are a few people that were given many dreams and the understanding of them.

Here is the list: Jacob (2) Joseph (6) in Genesis, then Daniel (3), and here in the Gospel is Joseph (4).

There are people God uses in this area. Some people discount dreams because they do not understand them, however, that does not mean that are not to be understood. Those that lack knowledge and understanding of dreams can study the subject just as in anything else which we do not know.

Dream 16

Joseph's First Recorded Dream

Observations:

- ➢ Joseph's personal concerns were addressed in the dream.

- ➢ God used a dream to explain how his virgin fiancé was pregnant.

- ➢ God gave instructions concerning the name of the child.

" But while he thought on these things, behold, the angel of the Lord appeared unto him in a dream , saying, Joseph, thou son of David, fear not to take unto thee Mary thy wife: for that which is conceived in her is of the Holy Ghost. And she shall bring forth a son, and thou shalt call his name JESUS: for he shall save his people from their sins. Now all this was done, that it might be fulfilled which was spoken of the Lord by the prophet, saying, Behold, a virgin shall be with child,

Dream 16

Joseph's First Recorded Dream

and shall bring forth a son, and they shall call his name Emmanuel, which being interpreted is, God with us.   Then Joseph being raised from sleep did as the angel of the Lord had bidden him, and took unto him his wife: And knew her not till she had brought forth her firstborn son: and he called his name JESUS."
(Matt 1:20-25)

The sewing machine was invented from a dream

Dream 17

Wise men's Dream

Bible Reference: *Matt 2:12*

Dream Type: Warning Dream

God had given these men a dream, warning them not to return to King Herod.

Man has limited ability and knowledge, but God is unlimited. If we learn to walk with God, we can learn to trust Him and be free from certain fears that bind us.

Reliance upon mans ability should be at a minimum, we should be learning to trust in God more and more. The lives of these men depended on obeying a dream. This shows us how important dreams can be. These wise men really were wise.

Dream 17

Wise men's Dream

Observations:

➢ According to the record, God didn't explain everything in the dream; this is where they needed faith. Almost every dream needs to be mixed with faith.

➢ God warned man in order to spare them loss. In this case it was loss of life. It could have been disastrous if this dream was disregarded.

They may not have been told how to go back to their country, however they were told not to return to Herod.

"And being warned of God in a dream that they should not return to Herod, they departed into their own country another way."
(Matt 2:12)

Dream 18

Joseph's Second Dream

Bible Reference: *Matt. 2:13-14*

Dream Type: Direction Dream

Seemingly, God gives certain (Direction) dreams to those who have the authority and or influence in a situation.

In this case, it was the husband who is the biblical head of the family. In Some cases, a dream may be given to a leader or someone who has influence over others.

This also emphasizes the importance of being in submission to those whom are appointed over us. God has an order to things.

Dream 18

Joseph's Second Dream

Observations:

- The dream was in reaction to the plan of an evil man, King Herod.

- The dream contained important information

- The dream included others, and affected others.

- The dream included timing.

"And when they were departed, behold, the angel of the Lord appeareth to Joseph in a dream , saying, Arise, and take the young child and his mother, and flee into Egypt, and be thou there until I bring thee word: for Herod will seek the young child to destroy him. When he arose, he took the young child and his mother by night, and departed into Egypt:"
(Matt. 2:13-14)

Dream 19

Joseph's Third Dream

Bible Reference: *Matt 2:19-23*

Dream Type: Direction Dream

Dreams can alter our plans simply because some things that are out of our control are constantly changing.

God can use dreams to changes our place of living or place of employment or place of worship.

Being flexible is a good thing in most cases. Seek the guidance of God in every situation, He is able to direct.

" The steps of a good man are ordered by the LORD: and he delighteth in his way."   (Ps 37:23)

Dream 19

Joseph's Third Dream

Observations:

- ➢ Directions that came through a dream, dispelled personal fears

- ➢ The dream came to the Father, concerning the family.

- ➢ The dream did not specify where Joseph was to relocate too exactly, but a general area. God works with the individual will of a person, so it will not seem as if God is treating them as a slave or robot.

"But when Herod was dead, behold, an angel of the Lord appeareth in a dream to Joseph in Egypt, Saying, Arise, and take the young child and his mother, and go into the land of Israel: for they are dead which sought the young child's life. And he arose, and took the young child and his mother, and came into the land of Israel." (*Matt 2:19-23*)

Dream 20

Joseph's Fourth Dream

Bible Reference: *Matt.2:22-23*

Dream Type: Warning Dream

Understanding dreams can help us with, understanding why we need to do a certain thing in a certain way at a certain time. Man has been given the ability to reason, which can be both beneficial and detrimental, depending on when we use it.

"Trust in the LORD with all thine heart; and lean not unto thine own understanding. In all thy ways acknowledge him, and he shall direct thy paths."(Prov 3:5-6)

It would be to our benefit to learn not to put all our trust in reason but in God and try to understand the different ways God uses to lead us; in this case it is through dreams.

Dream 20

Joseph's Fourth Dream

We should always obey God rather than man, or mans reasoning. A current word from God should take precedence over any knowledge we may have, this requires faith in God. The more we exercise our faith in what God communicates to us, the greater our faith will grow.

Observations:

- ➢ The dream must have contained a warning to him, not to settle in Judaea.

- ➢ Returning from Egypt was no short distance. They had to pass through Judaea to get to Galilee. This shows Joseph obedience to the dream.

- ➢ The dream may have allowed for personal choice to be made concerning where specifically to live.

Dream 20

Joseph's Fourth Dream

"But when he heard that Archelaus did reign in Judaea in the room of his father Herod, he was afraid to go thither: notwithstanding, being warned of God in a dream , he turned aside into the parts of Galilee: And he came and dwelt in a city called Nazareth: that it might be fulfilled which was spoken by the prophets, He shall be called a Nazarene."
(Matt.2:22-23)

" Then Peter and the other apostles answered and said, We ought to obey God rather than men."

Acts 5:29

Dream 21

Pilate's Wife Dream

Bible Reference: *Matt 27:17-19*

Dream Type: Prophetic Dream

This dream was not totally disclosed, however, we know who it was about, Jesus.

Notice that the dream was not given to Pilate that we know of, yet his wife was moved by it.

She did receive the dream and was affected by it. She tried to influence her husband to act on it as well but he chose not to. The dream came to someone who could influence the situation in this case it was Pilate's wife. Not everyone will share in your acceptance of your dreams.

Dream 21

Pilate's Wife Dream

Observations:

- The dream was given to Pilate's wife concerning Jesus.

- The truth of the dream was experienced by her. (That just man)

- The dream may have contained other predicted events that unfolded that very day. (suffered many things)

" Therefore when they were gathered together, Pilate said unto them, Whom will ye that I release unto you? Barabbas, or Jesus which is called Christ? For he knew that for envy they had delivered him. When he was set down on the judgment seat, his wife sent unto him, saying, Have thou nothing to do with that just man: for I have suffered many things this day in a dream because of him." (Matt. 27:19)

Part III

Dream

Dictionary

Launch Pad

Google was started from a dream

This last section is a personal compilation of some dream terms and definitions that I have learned over the years.

It is extremely important to remember that each dream has its own theme or message. Therefore, the same object appearing in different dreams may have different meanings or no meaning at all.

This dictionary of terms is only a launch pad, meaning, it is designed to help broaden your understanding of what the term can mean. You are encouraged to record your own terms. Starting a personal dream dictionary can help you for years to come.

There may be no meaning at all to certain items in your dreams it all depends on the context of the dream. If you take the time to write your dreams down, God sees that you value your dream and will give you more.

We are to seek God for his help in understanding dreams. We have taught dream interpreting to many people and the results have been consistently amazing.

God gives ideas concerning inventions in dreams; these are called:

Invention Dreams

Animals

In

Dreams

Animals in Dreams

Animals usually represent personal characteristics, but they also can use its name as a double meaning.
Example: Boar = Bore (To be disinterested)

Alligator – Gossiping spirit, big tail (Tale) and a big mouth, very dangerous

Baby Dragon- Low level demon

Badger- Agitator

Bees – Pest demons, spiritual pests, brings hurt, stings, distracts from our mission

Big Snake – Powerful Lie (Tale)

Boar – Boring, not exciting

Deer – Skittish, not trusting, loving, something dear to us.

Dove – A gentle one, Holy Spirit

Dragon – Satan, high level demonic power

Frogs- Demonic spirits, Rev.:16:13-14

Animals in Dreams

Horse- A means of delivery, strong in means. Physical power

Lion – Powerful, courageous, intimidator, man eater, destroyer, the devil

Little Snake – A newly formed lie, not much strength

Long Snake – A lie that has been around a very long time.

Mean Dog – A friend that turns on us.

Mosquito – Energy suckers, things that suck the life out of you.

Nice Dog – Friend, companion

Otter – Likes to slide, lazy, playful, not serious

Porpoise- Represents a purpose

Puppy – A new friend

Python – Constrictor, slowly squeezes the spirit out of you (This type of snake has camouflage spots and moves slow).

Snake – Lies, tails (tales)

Animals in Dreams

To Be Snake bitten- means we have accepted the lie. It affected us

Vipers – Hateful lies, bitterness, venomous

White Snake – Religious lie, hypocrisy

Tip: Dreams that show us ourselves are called:

Self Awareness Dreams

Areas

In

Dreams

Areas in Dreams

Areas –Usually represents a time of your life, also may represent a position, or view point.

A Street- a specific time of life

Along the Road- stationary place in life, temporary stop. Others may pass you by

Back door leading to backyard - you are opening up things from your past

Back Yard – Things in your past

Basement- The place of the foundation, the foundational elements of something

Bathroom- A place of personal cleansing, a place where you see yourself, a place to get rid of personal defilement

Behind Closed Door- Things hidden from others, made private

Bright Light- God's will, Gods presence

Close- Things close to happening, soon, things close to you

Areas in Dreams

Closed Door- Opportunity now closed, over

Darkness- Spiritual danger zone

Desert- Place of spiritual dryness

Distant- Things won't happen for a while yet, or happened long ago

Farm Field- A place of growth

Front of house looking into front yard- seeing things in your future

Front Yard – Things in your future

Hallway- place of transition, place requiring faith

Higher lever- Higher in influence or what the dream is suggesting

Highway- things are moving faster, accomplishing more

Living room- Where you live mostly

Lower level- Lower is less of something.

Office- A professional position, business life

Areas in Dreams

Open Door- Opportunity, (Exterior door) will be seen by others,(Interior door) will be seen by you

Playground- place of play, not taken things seriously

Rising above, flying – Rising in spiritual things and gifts

Road- your life time, the route you are on, also can be a general setting

Rooms- Areas in your life, position of occupancy

Woods- Place of growing leaders/strong believers, an undeveloped area, wild

Tip: If the dream can still remain without us in it then the dream is probably not about us. If we are involved in the dream then it is probably about us.

" For God speaketh once, yea twice, yet man perceiveth it not. In a dream, in a vision of the night, when deep sleep falleth upon men, in slumberings upon the bed;"

" Then he openeth the ears of men, and sealeth their instruction, That he may withdraw man from his purpose, and hide pride from man. He keepeth back his soul from the pit, and his life from perishing by the sword." (Job 33:14-18)

Body Parts In Dreams

Body Parts in Dreams

Body Parts – Represent close to what they do in the natural, their function.

Eyes – Look into, observe, Color may also be a factor.

Eyes like a cat, pupils are sideways slits – Spiritual Perception

Big Eyes – Spiritual vision, visions in the spirit.

Hair – Thought, wisdom, symbolic of what comes out of our mind.

Lame- spiritually crippled, needing a healing

Long hair – Long time thinker, wisdom, mature

Short hair – Short time thinker, wisdom, immature

Matted hair- unkempt, laziness, slept on.

Right Hand – Communion with God

Body Parts in Dreams

Left Hand – Our calling, vocation

Skinny Person- needing spiritual food/meat.

Teeth – Understanding, the ability to grasp comprehend a matter

Teeth falling out- Symbolic of time for growth into more mature or deeper spiritual material, needing a challenge.

Foot/Feet- what we stand on, our security, footing. Slippery would indicate insecurity, or not a good rule to trust in.

Tip: Dream Interpreting involves two main areas:
- Skill
- Revelation.

Skill can be acquired, but revelation only comes from God. As we read and study about dreams, Pray that God will help you learn and open up your understanding.

Buildings And Places In Dreams

Buildings and Places in Dreams

Buildings- Usually represent things we build on, or live in every day, a life. Seek to convert objects to the spiritual realm. Ask yourself what does this do? Then apply it spiritually.

Airport- a place of spiritual transition, air is usually symbolic of the spiritual realm, an object ascending in the air is something that is going higher in the spiritual realm, if it's descending it is going down in spiritual power and influence.

Apartment- a temporary place in your life, complacency

Auto Dealership – A place of starting new ministries, changing

Basement- hidden place; not seen by everyone; the place where the foundation is found

Bus Station – Short term destiny, a place where you get on and off at.

Carport- to Park temporarily

Church - Your spiritual life

Buildings and Places in Dreams

Courthouse- Heavenly court, a place concerning God's laws, very legal area

Deli- what we are feeding on. Place of feeding, symbolic of a church, spiritual food

Dusty Warehouse - A place that stores things that have not been used in a very long time

Forest- A place among leaders, undeveloped area, wild

Foundation- What we trust in, believe

Garage- Personally Parked, Idleness

Hospital- A place to help you heal. Symbolic of a Church

Hotel – A short term stay, only visiting

House - Your family, family life

Mall - Your business life

Mountain- God, a high place, very secure

Parking Lot- Not going anywhere, it's parked.

Buildings and Places in Dreams

Tall building- High anointing on your life, life elevated above the norm. Having a prominence seen by all

Train Station- Place of ministry transition longer time

Two story building - Has a higher level of spirituality

Warehouse - A place of supply, lots of, or storage.

Tip: Not every dream has an interpretation.

Colors

In

Dreams

Colors in Dreams

Color   P   Positive Meaning   Vivid colors

            N   Negative Meaning Muted colors

While colors do have meaning, colors may not have significance at all in certain dreams. It depends on the dream.
Learn to be flexible with dream data and definitions, this is not meant to be applied to every dream. Rather it is to provide a spring board to stimulate your mind to think in this area. And pray.

Red

P   Power, Redemption, Anointing

N   Anger, War, Destruction

Brown

P   Pastoral Care, Nurturing, Compassion

N   Humanism

Colors in Dreams

Blue

P   Revelation, Communion, Higher Authority   Ez 23;6

N   Emotional Lows

Gold/Amber

P   Holy, Hallowed

N   Greed

Purple

P   Authority, wealthy

N   Ungodly Authority

Orange

P   Perseverance

N   Stubbornness

Colors in Dreams

Yellow

P   the Mind

N   Fear, Lack of Courage

Pink

Combination of Red and White

Grey

Maturity

Green

P   Tenderness, Flexible, Life

N   Ignorant, unlearned, envious

Colors in Dreams

White

P   Righteousness, purity

N   Religious Spirit, hypocrisy

Scarlet

Opulence

Black

Official, death, satanic

Black and White

Very plain, easy to see and understand (There it is in black and white)

Tip: Some dreams have a delayed interpretation.

Garments In Dreams

Garments in Dreams

Garments may symbolize what a person appears to be, or is seen as being.

Armor- Battle Ready

Clothed in dust or dirt- Carnality, defilement

Coats of skin- Bare necessities

Colorful Garment, - Praise, glorifying to God

Diaper- Personal Defilement

Filthy Garment- Defilement, involved in sinful activities, unrepentant

House- Our physical body renewed

Kingly Robes- Authority

Long White garment-Angelic, holy life, sinless

Naked- Exposed, Vulnerable   Heb. 4:13

Robe of fine clean linen-Righteousness/Godly

Robe- Priestly, salvation

Sackcloth/ Burlap- Humility or repentance

Garments in Dreams

Strange Garments- Outside of Gods will

Underwear-Honesty, nothing hidden, full disclosure

Woolen- Outside of God's presence

Dream Example:

In the dream, I and this other man were cleaning up at a machine shop; I said to the man: did you know that there are twenty different categories of dreams? He put up his hand in a stopping motion and said: save your breath man, I'm not interested, then walked away, the dream was over.

I woke up and asked the Lord what was that about? The Lord answered and said:

" Not everyone will share your excitement."

Numbers

In

Dreams

Numbers in Dreams

Numbers- May represent a length of time, as in years, days, months. The numbers must go along with the context of the dream. (Gen.40)

1. New Life, Unity
2. Faithful Witness
3. Godhead, Resurrection, Fullness
4. Creation (4 direction, seasons, gospels)
5. Grace/Power to get past something (5 smooth stones)
6. Carnal, Incompleteness, Getting over issues common to mankind
7. Completeness (7 vials, trumpet, days of creation)
8. New Beginning, Resurrection
9. (Two meanings for 9)
Positive meaning: Fruit Bearing
Negative meaning: Judgment against the kingdom of darkness, carnality, spiritual realm

Numbers in Dreams

10. Perfect Order (10 Commandments)

11. Positive meaning: Heroes rising, Negative meaning: disorder
Also: The 11th hour would symbolize time is almost up.

12. Perfect government, under Gods control (12 tribes, and 12 months)

13. Rebellion

14. Generational Promises. (Matt. 1)

15. Consecration

16. Love of God

17. Overcoming power

18. Bondage

19. Faith

20. Expectancy; the currency of prophetic people

24. Completed cycle (One full day)

Numbers in Dreams

25. Begin

29. Mountain, high place, (Mt. Everest is 29029 feet high.)

153. Kingdom multiplication, (153 fishes)

666. Complete lawlessness

Double use of a word or term, usually means: The Thing Is Sure.

(Verily, verily)

Triple use of a word or term usually means: Excessive.

(Holy, holy, holy or Woe, woe, woe)

Objects

In

Dreams

Objects in Dreams

Objects – Mainly symbolize what they do. Ask yourself what does this object do, what is it's primary function.

Air Hose – Our connection with God, The Holy Spirit

Chalk board- Something to learn by.

Coffin or casket- Represents something dead

Decaying Tree- A person in spiritual decay, lacking

Electrical Cord – Our connection the God, The Holy Spirit power

Electrical Outlet- Some power being let out here, spiritual power

Fruit bearing Tree- Those that produce spiritual fruit

Guitar- Joyfulness, joy

Guitar without strings- Music without joy, carnal

Objects in Dreams

Light- What is shined out, something that illuminates, exposes.

Mirror – A reflection of you, self observation

Motorized Pallet Jack - Someone that bears up very heavy burdens, very spiritual person, lots of energy, strong

Pallet Jack- Someone that lifts up others on a small scale

Pieces – Small parts of something

Plant with leaves and no fruit- Those that appear to be godly but do not possess godliness of character.

Playing cards, Joker – A unpredictable person, someone that causes trouble

Price tags- Symbolic of what it will cost you to have. (Hardship, pain, suffering...)

Real Estate Sign: For sale, available for purchase

Rock – Eternal, unmovable, solid footing

Objects in Dreams

Tall Trees- Very influential leaders

Tapestry- A display of your life for all to see

Toilet- Personal defilement discarded here

Trees- Leaders, those of great strength, influence

Violin- Heavenly, sweetness

Weeds- Things that choke out the word of God, time consumers, time wasters.

Wire - stiffness, also a conductor of current, power, spiritual connection.

Bridge - A point of transition, crossing over into something new.

People

In

Dreams

People in Dreams

People – Represent what we know them for or as.

Co worker – Fellow laborer in Christ, or at our work

Doctor- One who helps us get better.

Driver – The leader of a ministry, the one we are allowing to influence us.

Faceless person – The Holy Spirit, we can't see but He helps us.

Father – Heavenly Father, Authority

Hunter- Someone that is hunting for something

Invisible passenger giving directions and assistance- The Holy Spirit

Judge- One who sits in judgment of another, critical, God, the law

Killer- One who kills, devil

People in Dreams

Mother – Nurturer, guidance giver, what was your mom known to you as?

Old Friend – Old life before salvation

Passenger in vehicle – Those involved with a ministry or influence

Pastor – God, Divine authority

Police Officer – The law, law of God

Real Estate Agent – Jesus our go between, agent on our side, our representative

Thief- One who steals, devil

Note: Handel's Messiah was said to be written from a dream

Vehicles

In

Dreams

Vehicles in Dreams

Vehicles- Mainly represent realms of influence, ministries, the larger the vehicle, the larger the realm of influence or ministry.

Airplane – A very spiritual ministry or person

Ascending Airplane- A spiritual Ministry taking off, growing, increasing in spiritual life

Bicycle – One man ministry, on their own.

Bulldozer - A very pushy/ dominant person

Car -   Local Ministry

City Bus - City Wide Ministry

Descending Airplane- A ministry that is decreasing in spiritual life.

Flat Tire on a vehicle – Ministry operating on very little Holy Spirit Power. Needs more prayer.

Foreign markings on Airplane – A ministry that is foreign to us. We don't understand it.

Vehicles in Dreams

Fork Lift- One who picks others up on a professional level. Also bears a tremendous load

Go Cart- Not taking your influence seriously, selfish, immature

Hearse- Represents a funeral, something dead or something that has died

Helicopter- Small private unique ministry very spiritual

Jumbo Airplane- Large spiritual ministry

Airborne Mothership – Demonic stronghold over an area

Motor home – The Family in motion, action/activities involving them all.

Muscle Car- Older but very powerful ministry

Ocean Liner – International Ministry

Pick Up Truck – Encouragement to others, Picks them up.

Rescue Boat- Ministry that helps the hurting

Vehicles in Dreams

School Bus- Encourage learners, picks up students, involving students

Small Airplane- Small spiritual ministry,

Space ship – Out of this world- Very Spiritual

Tricycle - A very immature position.

Van - Larger local ministry, more influence than a car

A Slow Moving Vehicle in front of you on the road- Something that is slowing you down from reaching your destiny

Tip: Fear Dreams and Calling Dreams are often reoccurring

Dreams may also explain a situation

Water

In

Dreams

Water in Dreams

Water- Is used for washing away of something, used for spiritual cleansing from sin or defilements. Also describes the word of God.

Shower – Cleansing your body from impurities and habits that are harmful.

Sink- Cleansing your appearance, how you see yourself.

River- Boundaries, mighty in power or effect

Ocean – Large area of Humanity (a sea of people)

Lake- smaller area of humanity, local

Rain – Needed for growth

Flood- Unstoppable, oversupply, abundant

Toilet- Place of carnal refuse, hidden attitudes that need to go.

Pipe - Symbolic of a person or method that channels something.

Running water- Symbolic of a constant supply of grace to remove sinfulness.

Write your dreams down and review them often

Note: The young man Albert Einstein is said to have received the theory of relativity in 19 consecutive dreams.

Other Elements In Dreams

Other Elements

Time piece- Time is limited, or of importance

Hole through outside wall- illegal access occurring, area that is accessible to the enemy

Landscaping in front of a home- things that are growing for all to see.

Flying in the air- very spiritual, air is symbolic of spirit.

Cloud - People around you, those who witness your life.

Reusable lumber- helping former church members become useful again.

The End

"Where there is no vision, the people perish:"
Prov. 29:18

IN CASE YOU ARE WONDERING HOW YOU CAN GET CLOSER TO GOD; HERE IS A PRAYER THAT YOU CAN PRAY:

PRAYER:

Lord Jesus, I admit that I am a sinner and I need to be forgiven of all my sins. I believe you died on the cross and have been raised from the dead. I now surrender my life into your hands. Please forgive me, come into my heart, and fill me with your Holy Spirit that I may live for you.

Amen.

Obtaining Biblical Dream Language Definitions

In this chapter I want to show you that there are places in the bible that have definitions pertaining to dream interpreting.

Both Old and New Testaments contain elements of information for the understanding of our dreams.

We want to make you aware of them so you can notice them as you read your bible.

We will have a brief bible study as we use the term dragon for an example:

Dragon

Before we get into the bible verses we want to highlight a fundamental step and that is simply asking the question:

What does a dragon symbolize?

Here's a bit of knowledge I have learned from God for interpreting dreams and understanding their messages:

Ask yourself the question:

What does this element do? Or; what are its main characteristics?

In this case we are dealing with the term dragon; a dragon is commonly known as a fierce devourer, a predator, an unpredictable insubordinate serpent like figure, a dragon is not known to be gentle, loving or caring; with this in mind let's compare it to what the bible has to say about the dragon:

Dragon

Reading in the book of Revelation chapter 12 verse 9:

"And the great dragon was cast out, that old serpent, called the Devil, and Satan..."

That is a definition of the dragon; it's the devil also known as Satan.

That makes total sense because the devil is known for being a predator, unpredictable, insubordinate and having the characteristics of a serpent.

We also come across another reference to the dragon in Revelation chapter 20:

"And I saw an angel come down from heaven, having the key of the bottomless pit and a great chain in his hand and he laid hold on the dragon , that old serpent, which is the Devil, and Satan, and bound him a thousand years," (Revelation 20:1-2)

The bible has made is clear what a dragon symbolizes; the devil, Satan or connected to Satan.

Waters

Here is another element found in scripture: Sea

"And he saith unto me, The waters which thou sawest, where the whore sitteth, are peoples, and multitudes, and nations, and tongues."

(Revelation 17:15)

Using these scriptures we have found the definition of a few dream elements. There are a few unbiblical methods of dream interpreting out there however the bible is the one true source for helping us determine the meaning of our dreams. We hope this book has helped you get started in understanding your dreams.

Dream Example:

In the dream I was with a small group of people entering into a warehouse filled with old tools and equipment, the lighting was dingy and old, I left the group and went in between the racks to a work bench that was against the wall, I spotted an old violin case and went to it; I opened the dusty case and there was a very old violin inside, the name on the tattered case was BRUNO. I had no idea what it was worth but I wanted it; I brought it over to the group that was standing in the center aisle and laid it on a table; I opened it and showed the leader what I found, then asked if I may keep it, he looked at the violin and displayed no interest at all and replied: sure. The dream was over.

1. The dream was about me and the group I was currently involved with

2. I found something that had been stored for a long time

3. The leader was not interested in what I found

4. I looked up the name Bruno and to my surprise it was a real violin manufacturer that crafted very expensive and rare violins.

5. Dream interpreting was this rare find, I had been excited to discover it and others were not interested in it; but to me it was very valuable.

Printed in Great Britain
by Amazon